THE DISTORTION OF FACTS IN THE DIGITAL AGE

LARRY GERBER

rosen publishing's
rosen central®

New York

Published in 2013 by The Rosen Publishing Group, Inc.
29 East 21st Street, New York, NY 10010

Library of Congress Cataloging-in-Publication Data

Gerber, Larry, 1946–
The distortion of facts in the digital age/Larry Gerber.—First edition.
        pages cm.—(Digital and information literacy)
Includes bibliographical references and index.
ISBN 978-1-4488-8357-8 (library binding)—
ISBN 978-1-4488-8368-4 (pbk.)—
ISBN 978-1-4488-8369-1 (6-pack)
1. Electronic information resource literacy–Juvenile literature. 2. Internet literacy—Juvenile literature. 3. Information literacy—Juvenile literature. 4. Deception—Juvenile literature. 5. Truthfulness and falsehood—Juvenile literature. 6. Mass media and children–Juvenile literature. I. Title.
ZA4065.G47 2013
025.04—dc23

2012024759

Manufactured in the United States of America

CPSIA Compliance Information: Batch #W13YA: For further information, contact Rosen Publishing, New York, New York, at 1-800-237-9932.

CONTENTS

INTRODUCTION

There's nothing new about twisting the truth. That kind of distortion has been around since people learned to lie. Today, however, the Internet moves words and pictures faster than ever, to more people than ever, making toxic information potentially more harmful than ever.

Distortion is also as new as the next idea. No matter where you go on the Web, it's a safe bet that somebody, somewhere, has figured out a new way to twist the truth to get what they want: people's money, their time, their vote, or their trust.

Fortunately the Internet can also deliver the antidote to distortion: facts. The challenge is finding them amid all the clutter. Search engines can help, but even the best ones can't tell the difference between truth and lies. A few Web sites specialize in doing just that, however. FactCheck.org and the NewsLiteracyProject.org are just two of the sites that can help to expose falsehoods and sort fact from fiction online. As you read on, you will also discover other reliable sites for information on all kinds of specific topics.

Seeing through distortion also means asking the right questions, usually some of the "Five Ws" (who, what, where, when, and why)

that reporters and researchers are trained to ask. You'll see a lot of those questions here. They're suggested as starting points for research as well as suggestions for sorting good information from bad.

They're especially important for people doing their own blogs or their own reporting. Opinion polls show that public trust in the traditional news media has been shrinking for years. At the same time, digital access for everybody means that everybody can be a news reporter. And that would be great, if everybody knew how to report news. Experts make it look easy; beginners often botch it. Reporters must know how to separate fact from opinion, distortion, and lies, and they usually don't have very much time to think about it. It takes practice.

Disinformation is like poison. Sometimes it acts quickly, sometimes slowly, but sooner or later it does damage. Whether you're doing research work, blogging, shopping, or deciding what to believe, it pays to recognize digital dishonesty and avoid it. Critical thinkers are hard to fool, and they are usually impossible to fool for very long.

The Internet can deliver bad information along with facts, but it also provides tools to help tell the difference. Asking a librarian is often a great time-saver.

It might sound like boring work, but tracking down facts through a jungle of distortion is actually one of the more entertaining games on the Web, and it's free. It can take time, so it helps to know shortcuts. You'll learn about several of them.

There's also discussion of political reporting and political language, but it's not intended to be about who's right and who's wrong. It is about recognizing the distortion that happens when people disagree about politics and other topics. Web sites are noted because many people have found them useful, not because of their politics, if any.

Chapter 1

What Is Disinformation?

here's a lot of bad information on the Internet, but not all of it is posted to fool people. Everybody makes mistakes, and those are called misinformation. Or just mistakes.

Disinformation is something else. It's false information that's spread in order to deceive. Sometimes it's done by skillful, well-paid experts, sometimes by people who can barely read and write. It's delivered by all kinds of messengers, from huge media corporations to obsessed bloggers who log a dozen visitors in a busy year.

Disinformation doesn't have to be an outright lie. It often works best when it's built around a grain of truth that's distorted somehow. Trivial facts may be reported in a way that makes them seem important, while significant facts are ignored or barely mentioned. "Distort" comes from a Latin word meaning "twist out of shape," and it comes from the same root as "torture." A more modern word is "spin," which means pretty much the same thing.

Distortion is often hard to see until its results appear, and they can be devastating. Half the Americans surveyed in a 2006 Harris Interactive

Disinformation thrives on conflict, particularly war. In times of stress and danger, people may feel that their cause is more important than the truth.

poll believed that Iraq had "weapons of mass destruction" (WMD) when the United States invaded in 2003. That's what they had been told by government leaders at the time. U.S. and international experts reported that Iraq had no such weapons, but they got less attention than the president, vice president, and other top officials who said otherwise.

The false WMD claims were echoed on the Internet and by other media. They were widely accepted by the public, and the government used them to justify the war. More than two thousand Americans were killed, and thousands more Iraqis died.

A sixteen-month investigation costing $900 million concluded that Iraq's nuclear, chemical, and biological weapons programs had been dismantled twelve years earlier. There was no WMD threat. Even today, however, many Americans still believe there was.

When people get fooled, they don't like to admit it. That's one of the things that makes distortion so effective. For lies to work, people have to be willing to accept them.

The Good, the Bad, the Commercial

Why do people go to the trouble to lie or distort when it's usually simpler to tell the truth? It would be easy to write off people who twist the truth as sick or evil, and some of them surely are. Racist hate sites are alive and well all over the Web. Some of the commentary posted by big corporate media feeds racial mistrust.

The Southern Poverty Law Center (http://www.splcenter.org) keeps track of online haters, both the openly rabid ones and the talking heads of commercial radio and television who are sneakier about their racism.

However, a lot of distortion is just business as usual, and that's not totally terrible. Many people think of propaganda as something evil or dishonest, but it doesn't have to be. Propaganda is just information that promotes a certain point of view. The most common propaganda in America is advertising.

Most people expect some exaggeration or distortion in ads. There's nothing wrong with promoting a product or putting an agreeable face on an election candidate. The problems arise when the promoters are dishonest and when people make decisions—to buy a product or vote for a candidate—based on falsehood.

Some people become so obsessed with an issue that they'll say just about anything to make their point about it. "Crank" sites are all over the Web. Some people just like to spread gossip, rumors, and lies without bothering to find out the truth or caring about it. As often as not, they're feeding their own resentments or prejudices.

But there are also plenty of otherwise honest folks who seem to feel that some things— such as God, country, or family—are more important

This billboard in Colorado questions President Barack Obama's U.S. citizenship and suggests he is a Muslim. It also hints that he was involved in a fatal shooting at Fort Hood, Texas.

than inconvenient facts. They may feel that it's OK to pass on bad information as long as it serves their higher cause.

Politics and Other Conflicts

Political campaigns generate distortion of all kinds, particularly when candidates attack each other through ads and planted disinformation. In 2008, bloggers and e-mailers fueled the "birther" movement, claiming President Barack Obama was born outside the United States

File   Edit   View   Favorites   Tools   Help

DON'T LET DISINFORMATION GET PERSONAL

Don't Let Disinformation Get Personal

Scammers prowl communities like Facebook looking for victims or use e-mail to hoodwink people out of money. Sex predators may hide behind phony Internet identities.

If disinformation is directed at you personally—as in an e-mail—be very careful! The basic safety rule is the following: don't give out any personal information unless you're opening an account with a company you know, on a site you know is secure. (Look for the "locked" icon on your browser's address bar.) The National Cyber Security Alliance (http://staysafeonline.org) is one of many useful safety sites. It covers things from identify theft to Facebook privacy settings.

Shaky medical and drug information can be particularly dangerous, for obvious reasons. Health on the Net Foundation lists advice Web sites that pass its eight-point code of conduct (http://www.hon.ch/HONcode/Conduct.html). It may be helpful to look up symptoms, but it's a terrible idea to take medications or avoid seeing a doctor based on information you find on the Web.

and therefore could not legally serve as president. Commercial media producers liked the story and kept it alive, even after publication of the president's birth certificate and other documents showed the claims were bogus.

The presidential campaign of 2004 featured attacks on the military records of both candidates, John Kerry and George W. Bush. Kerry, who served honorably in Vietnam, was smeared on grounds he later opposed that war. The attackers were discredited, but Kerry lost the election. CBS newsman Dan Rather resigned after some of his source documents were challenged as fake. Rather had used the documents for a story claiming that Bush skipped out on his National Guard duty.

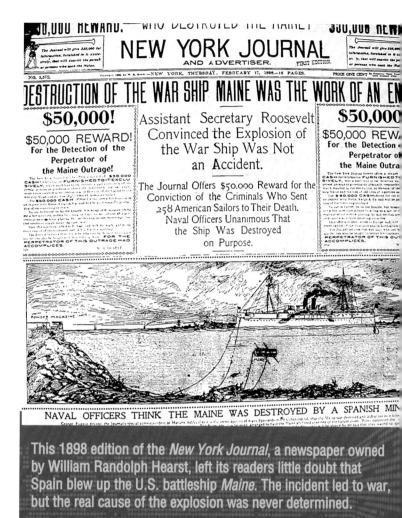

This 1898 edition of the *New York Journal*, a newspaper owned by William Randolph Hearst, left its readers little doubt that Spain blew up the U.S. battleship *Maine*. The incident led to war, but the real cause of the explosion was never determined.

Disinformation thrives around conflict, and war is the biggest conflict. "All warfare is based on deception," Chinese strategist Sun Tzu wrote 2,400 years ago. In today's democracies, leaders who favor war often must persuade many of their own people to go along with them in fighting one.

The second Iraq war wasn't the only U.S. conflict to get started with a disinformation campaign. Others include the Spanish-American

War of 1898 and the Vietnam War. Both involved alleged—claimed but not proved—attacks on U.S. Navy ships. Both "attacks" got big-headline media coverage that fanned public opinion for war. Much of the coverage turned out to be wrong.

The Spanish-American War is regarded today as history's first media-generated war. It was stirred up by millionaires William Randolph Hearst and Joseph Pulitzer to sell more newspapers. Media billionaire Rupert Murdoch of Australia played a similar role in the second Iraq war. His Fox News broadcast "mass destruction" scare propaganda as if it were fact and ignored or attacked those who presented facts showing it was wrong. Other companies repeated the WMD propaganda as well. Some of them later admitted they should have tried harder to find the facts.

Chapter 2

Masters of Hate

A demagogue is a public figure who attracts a mass following by appealing to some of the most basic human emotions: fear, hate, anger, resentment, greed, or vanity. Those can be troublesome feelings, and demagogues can be troublesome characters. Many of history's great demagogues were masters of distortion and hate speech.

"Demagogue" is often misused as a common political slur. To see how, use it in a search, plus the name of just about any popular leader who has enemies. Political views, even extreme ones, don't make a demagogue; neither does popularity, controversy, or name-calling by one's opponents. Demagogues are defined by their methods.

How Demagogues Operate

Fear, anger, and other negative emotions need a target, so many demagogues try to focus people's attention on an enemy, an "other" who can be blamed for society's troubles.

File   Edit   View   Favorites   Tools   Help

1984

1984

George Orwell's novel *1984* is set in a dystopia, a future society where things have gone terribly wrong. Published in 1949, it describes a man's efforts to find truth and love under the eyes of "Big Brother." The head of the ruling Party controls everything, even people's thoughts.

The main character of *1984*, Winston Smith, lives in Oceania, where disinformation rules. People use an invented language—Newspeak—so they can talk "correctly" about what's happening. Newspeak makes it impossible to have unapproved thoughts.

Newspeak twists meaning backward. Smith works in the Ministry of Truth, which specializes in lies. There's a Ministry of Love, where people are tortured and brainwashed. Oceania is always at war, and wars are directed by the Ministry of Peace. Newspeak doesn't have a word for "science," because science requires critical thinking. That's a thought-crime, and the thought police are never far away.

To stay out of trouble, people in Oceania practice doublethink. If the Party says black is white, it's not enough to say simply black is white. People must truly believe it. They must forget that they ever thought otherwise.

Orwell's world is extreme, but readers of *1984* can find disturbing similarities to current events. Governments and powerful institutions do try to control thought by twisting the meaning of words. Many people do practice a form of doublethink—holding on to an idea even when it's contradicted by obvious facts.

Today, the word "Orwellian" is used to describe total government control, extreme disinformation, and self-deception.

German dictator Adolf Hitler (1889–1945) is widely viewed as history's worst demagogue. He preached hatred of gays, Gypsies (Romani), intellectuals, and others, but his main target was Jews. They were persecuted and eventually murdered by the millions. Today, comparing an opponent to Hitler is one of the most common Web insults.

In the 1930s, Father Charles Coughlin, a Canadian-born Roman Catholic priest, became America's most popular radio commentator. He drew millions of listeners by taking the side of the poor and unemployed. He also incited his audiences against the governing "elite," rich bankers, and Jews.

Coughlin liked the fascist ideas of Hitler in Germany and Benito Mussolini (1883–1945), the ruler of Italy. As the United States approached war with those dictatorships, Coughlin lost his broadcasters and his audience. He is known today as "the father of hate radio."

Adolf Hitler, who salutes members of the Hitler Youth organization in 1936, used lies and distortion to rally German support for his dictatorship. He preached hatred of Jews and other "enemies," leading to millions of deaths.

Demagogues tend to rise when times are uncertain and people feel threatened. The threat may be imaginary or exaggerated, but often it's real. When Coughlin preached and Hitler came to power in the 1930s, the world was reeling from economic collapse and mass unemployment.

During the Cold War of the 1950s, mass media taught Americans to fear the Communist Soviet Union and its nuclear weapons. Republican senator Joseph McCarthy made headlines and gained political power by accusing his enemies of being spies and Communists. He held hearings that amounted to witch hunts of people in government and the army. Many victims lost their jobs or were persecuted in other ways. After four years of unfounded charges, McCarthy was publicly shamed and disciplined by the Senate, then suffered a demagogue's nightmare: being ignored.

Senator Joseph McCarthy, a demagogue of the 1950s, gained political power by playing on Americans' fear of Communism. He is seen here during a broadcast of the CBS TV show *Face the Nation* in 1954.

Just Plain Folks

Demagogues often portray themselves as just plain folks, trying to protect decent people from the evil "others." Some play the clown or the dunce, and their antics often appeal to people who feel inferior to the rich or well educated. Mussolini strutted and posed for pictures in comic-opera costumes.

Demagogues need mass media, and many have been skilled public speakers. Before the

Commentator Glenn Beck left Fox News in 2011 after people took to the streets and the Internet to protest his remarks about blacks, Hispanics, gays, and other minorities.

Internet, they usually needed money or powerful connections to get on radio or television. Today, the Web makes life easy for them. For obvious reasons, they can exist only in societies that allow freedom of speech.

Judging by comments on talk radio and political blogs, demagogues and hate speech seem to be thriving in the United States. Many countries have laws against inciting race hatred or violence against groups in society. However, the First Amendment to the U.S. Constitution guarantees freedom of speech, and the government has always been reluctant to crack down even when talk turns cruel. Public pressure can take the place of government restriction, however.

In 2011, right-wing commentator Glenn Beck left Fox News after groups on the Web organized a boycott of his sponsors. Beck mocked and stereo-typed blacks, Jews, gays, Native Americans, Mexicans, and others. One Beck tactic was to accuse his targets, including President Obama, of racism.

Chapter 3

How Disinformation Works

utright lies such as hoaxes and scams are often easier to spot than clever distortions, which usually have an element of truth. And the most effective distortion is often the kind that's hard to see, even when everybody's watching.

Framing is a way of influencing the way people think by presenting information to them in a certain way. By making the "frame" a certain size, and holding it in a certain place, false media messengers show selected facts and hide others.

Imagine a TV crew showing up in a neighborhood for a live shot of something. People come outside to see what's going on. On the video feed, it might look like a mob has invaded. A person at the scene might see a street deserted, except for the twenty people waving at the camera.

Framing with words usually involves rhetoric, or language that's loaded with hidden meaning. Take, for example, "tax relief" vs. "fair taxes." The first is Republican-style rhetoric. Relief is something people seek from pain or stress. It implies that taxes are unbearably painful or

TV crews and rescue workers wait for victims of an explosion that was reported on a yacht off the coast of New Jersey in 2012. It sounded like a big story, but it turned out to be a hoax.

stressful. The second is more likely Democratic rhetoric. It implies that some people aren't paying their fair share, and that they should.

That kind of shorthand can be useful for putting complicated ideas into a couple of words. It tells you right away where the speaker's coming from. But it can also be misused for distortion or coded hate speech, for example when people use "Muslims" and "terrorists" as if they meant the same thing, or mention San Francisco as a reference to gays. Code phrases that touch on people's race, religion, sexual orientation, or home backgrounds are plain signals of dishonesty. Why speak in code unless you have a message to hide?

False balance is another way to frame issues. It's what happens when media present very different positions as though they were similar. Let's say a Web site hosts a debate between Candidate A, who says the state needs better roads and schools, and Candidate B, who wants to evacuate the state because the Earth is flat and it's about to tip, spilling everyone off one side. What's the audience supposed to think? That the truth is somewhere in between?

The site is being dishonest. Just by hosting the debate, it forces rational Candidate A into the same frame as loony Candidate B. It makes B seem a bit more rational, and A a bit more loony. The debate is set up to look balanced, but it's way off balance. The site definitely favors B, whether it says so or not.

False balance and personal attacks are examples of fallacies, or mistakes in logic. Fallacies are ways people get misled to the wrong conclusions even though they may have all the facts. Some critical thinking sites list more than one hundred known fallacies, but most of those are variations on twenty or so main ones.

On the Web, a favorite flamer fallacy is ad hominem. It means personally attacking an opponent to avoid dealing with his or her argument. For example: "You know nothing about basketball. You can't even speak good English!"

Begging the question is another common fallacy. It means putting your point in a question or statement as if it's a proven fact: "We need the death penalty to stop murderers" is one. It concludes that the death penalty stops murderers, without proving it. "When did you quit kicking your dog?" is another example. The question just assumes you're a pet abuser. It leaves no room for what might be the truth: "I never kicked my dog!"

Who's Fooling Whom?

It would be hard to get away with lying if people didn't make it easy for liars. In a way, it's only natural. In early childhood, kids pick up their

File　Edit　View　Favorites　Tools　Help

How Good News Is Written

Most mainstream news organizations have codes of conduct. The Society of Professional Journalists (SPJ) has a list of thirty-seven dos and don'ts that cover everything from taking bribes and plagiarism to making sure facts are checked. Deliberate distortion is the first "don't" on the list.

Sometimes journalists witness news firsthand. When they get information from others, they're supposed to let you know the source for every bit of it, except in one possible situation: a source won't talk unless his or her name is kept secret. Even then, the information can't be used unless it passes two more tests, according to Associated Press guidelines.

1. It must be fact, not opinion.
2. The information can't be found anywhere else.

Sometimes good reporters go even further, if they can, telling why the source won't talk on the record. Will he or she lose a job? Lose business? Get arrested? It could be important for the reader to know.

Next time you see information from an anonymous source, ask if it meets those conditions. All anonymous sourcing requires some explanation. If you don't see it, be alert for disinformation. (For the SPJ guidelines, see http://www.spj.org/ethicscode.asp.)

ideas about what's good or bad, right or wrong, tasteful or gross. For the rest of their lives, they're more likely to accept information that supports those ideas and to reject anything that doesn't. This tendency is called bias. People can get past their built-in biases by learning to think critically, but few are born with that ability.

Congresswoman Michele Bachmann of Minnesota got low credibility scores while campaigning for the 2012 Republican presidential nomination. The nonpartisan Web site PolitiFact graded 53 of her statements and found 72 percent of them to be mostly or totally false.

Seeing how much disinformation is out there, it's easy to cop a cynical attitude. Lots of people do. How often have you heard some version of: "You can't believe anything they say!" That's another false balance. There are a lot more honest reporters than reporters who distort the facts.

The words "cynical" and "skeptical" sometimes get confused, but they mean very different ways of thinking. A skeptic is someone who asks questions and draws conclusions from the answers. Skeptics never accept anything without examination, but they stay open to all possible results, and they try to set aside their own biases.

Cynics are all about prejudice, not in the racial sense but in the sense that they judge before the facts are in. They don't see much point in asking questions because they already know the answers will probably be lies. It's hard for true cynics to learn anything. A skeptic tries to keep an open mind; a cynic's mind is shut tight.

TEN GREAT QUESTIONS

TO ASK A LIBRARIAN

1. What are the best sites for information about my topic?

2. Are there any sites I should avoid because they're not reliable?

3. Is there material about this subject that might not be on the Web?

4. What are the names of some good sources I could search for information about this subject?

5. How can I tell whether this source is biased or not?

6. Where can I find other points of view about this information?

7. What are some good starting search terms to find information about this topic?

8. How can I refine this search to find the specific information I'm seeking?

9. Are there places I can search that don't come up on Google?

10. What are some good sites for video footage about this subject?

Chapter 4

A Closer Look at News

A fact is information that's true and can be proven true. An opinion is the belief that something is true, whether it really is true or not. Being able to see the difference is a big deal because facts and opinions don't often come in separately labeled bundles. They get all jumbled together, even when everybody's being honest. Dishonest messengers specialize in confusing the two.

Credible news sites are clear about which is which on their pages. They use heads like "editorials," "opinion," "analysis," or "op-ed," and their ads are clearly separated or labeled. Opinion has a way of sneaking in everywhere, however.

Reporters must choose the sources they use, and sometimes there are many to choose from. Sources may have widely different opinions. They may be honest, or they may be spinners.

Reliable reporters, editors, and producers try to choose sources who 1) know what they're talking about, 2) state facts accurately, and 3) are open about what they have to gain or lose by talking.

The *Philadelphia Inquirer* was sold in 2010 after declaring bankruptcy. Many respected newspapers have been sold, merged, or driven out of business in the past thirty years.

Fact or Opinion?

Let's look at this line from a made-up news story about a senator named Smith.

"Violent crime is getting out of hand," Smith said.

Is that fact or opinion?

The sentence has two parts. The main part is "Smith said." That's stated as fact by the writer. What about the crime part? It might be fact, but it sounds a lot like Smith's opinion. Smith gives no actual crime statistics, and "out of hand" could mean just about anything.

Does that mean it's disinformation? Not by itself. If the reporter is on the job, he or she has checked Smith's statement against the facts and put those in the story. If not, you're stuck with Smith's word for it. Or are you?

Search "crime statistics." The Federal Bureau of Investigation (FBI) keeps official ones, and so do state governments. If the numbers for the past few years are decreasing, then crime is not getting "out of hand." Why is Smith so worried about crime and not other problems? Hint: Could money be involved?

The Center for Responsive Politics keeps track of where politicians' money comes from at OpenSecrets.org. If Smith gets big donations from the private security industry—which stands to profit from people's fear of crime—then things start getting clearer. Smith's statement wasn't fact or opinion. It was probably disinformation. It looks like Smith has a conflict of interest.

How about the reporter who quoted Smith? Is he or she to be trusted? It's impossible to tell without reading the whole story, of course. But if the reporter failed to report Smith's private security connection, that byline might be a good one to skip in future search results.

Speaking of bylines: reliable Web sites identify their writers and say something about their qualifications. Exceptions may be one-person blogs or articles written by several people, which are credited to their organization. Otherwise, articles without bylines are automatically suspect.

Professional writers, reporters, and producers, as well as sources who are well-qualified in their fields, usually have little to gain by distorting, and a lot to lose. News reporters especially value credibility as their biggest asset. ("Credible" means "believable" or "trustworthy.") If people don't believe what a reporter says, he or she needs to look for a new job. Even a single "stretcher" can wreck a career.

Corrected mistakes can be signs of credibility. Ethical reporters and bloggers correct mistakes immediately and clearly, and good sites place

File   Edit   View   Favorites   Tools   Help

   WIKIPEDIA

Wikipedia

Wikipedia can be an excellent site to start research. Article footnotes often link to sources that can be cited, or named as sources in a paper or article. But if you're working on a research project, chances are the instructor has told you not to cite Wikipedia itself. Why not?

Just about anybody can write and edit Wikipedia articles. Spokesmen for government agencies, corporations, interest groups, political candidates, bands, movies, and all kinds of causes try to promote their products or points of view on one of the Web's most popular information sites. At any given time, a Wikipedia article may contain biased or downright bogus information.

Wikipedia volunteer editors put in thousands of hours checking article sources for reliability and discussing whether the wording of articles is accurate and unbiased, as required by Wikipedia's editorial guidelines.

But it can take time for disinformation or misinformation to come to their attention, and it can take even longer for contributors to agree on how to fix the problem material. Sometimes it takes a lot of debate.

Writers, editors, and public relations agents argue their points on discussion boards that are open for everyone to read. The arguments, sometimes friendly and constructive, sometimes hot and bitter, are similar to arguments between writers and editors in newsrooms.

corrections in a prominent place. Some sites try to cover up mistakes by rewriting without explaining. They score lower on the credibility scale. Sites where editors leave bad information hanging around have no credibility.

A teacher and student check out a blog at an Alaska high school computer class. Some people believe bloggers can do the job of professional journalists, but fair reporting isn't as easy as it might seem.

Paying for a Free Press

The news business was changing radically even before the creation of the Internet. For years, newspapers employed more reporters than all other media and covered stories in more places. Beginning in the 1980s, reporters lost jobs and news bureaus closed as papers went out of business, merged, or were bought by major corporations.

Before this time, most newspaper companies existed only to provide news. They naturally took care to preserve their credibility, and they taught

Students participate in a journalism workshop at *La Opinion* newspaper in Los Angeles, California. With help from advisers at the University of Southern California, they launched a newspaper in English and Spanish.

good practices to new reporters and editors. Today's newspapers—whether they're read online or on paper—still try to do those things. But today, the newspaper is likely just one of many properties owned by a giant corporation that has many other products. The owners may care more about profit than good news reporting, which is often expensive. Reporters who work for big organizations don't usually pick their own assignments. They cover what they're told, and just the fact that they're reporting it makes it news. Media owners hire the people who make those decisions, so they have enormous influence on public opinion. Yet their private interests are often hidden.

A lot of the information on "independent" sites and blogs comes from newspapers and other mainstream media. Wherever news comes from, it's a good idea to remember that just about everyone involved in producing it is looking for something in return. That's not necessarily bad. Most news in the United States is paid for by advertising. Ads may be annoying at times, but they pay the bills for news organizations to operate independently of government. The traditional role of a free press is to be the public's watchdog, calling down powerful people and institutions when they get out of line.

Some people believe the watchdog job can be handled today by independent bloggers and "citizen journalists," people who put their own news on a digital network. Anybody with information and Web access can be a citizen journalist. However, it takes practice and training to learn how to report accurately and fairly, and to avoid distortion. There are lots of training programs, but many efforts to teach digital journalism to citizen journalists have flopped for lack of interest. And money is always a challenge. Real reporting means going to where news happens, bringing the equipment to collect and send it, and hopefully finding a place to eat and sleep afterward. Many people feel journalism is too big a job to be treated as a hobby.

School journalism courses and professional internships are still some of the best places to learn. The News Literacy Project is just one of several groups that arrange classes, workshops, and newsroom visits for students. Meanwhile organizations like Global Post and Reader Supported News are working on new models for Internet news funded by subscribers. News organizations of all types encourage questions from online readers. Most reporters will gladly help students with questions, no matter how busy they are.

MYTHS&FACTS

MYTH The headline tells what's in a story.

FACT Headlines are useful to search engines, but not always to readers. They can be exaggerated or misleading, and they don't always reflect exactly what's in the story. Many of them aren't written by the reporter.

MYTH The media have a liberal (or conservative) bias.

FACT News generally focuses on change, and liberals generally favor change. Things that stay the same aren't news, and conservatives generally favor the status quo. That's not bias, just the nature of news. The opinions of most newsroom staffs are usually about the same mix as those of their communities.

MYTH News stories should be fair and balanced.

FACT Most people believe news stories should be fair. Balance is sometimes an illusion, and it can be unfair.

Chapter 5

On Site

Signs of distortion get easier to spot with practice, but it usually takes time to compare sources and track facts. And nobody likes to waste time wading through text or video only to discover that the information is worthless.

Searches and Sources

If you're looking at pages of search results, save time by checking each site's URL before going to the site. The three-letter uniform resource locator is the "dot-something" that indicates what kind of organization hosts the page.

Schools use .edu; governments in the United States use .gov. School-hosted information usually gets good grades for accuracy and a minimum of spin, although school sites are also notorious for prank and hoax pages. The information on many government sites is official, and there's a lot of it. Sites with .edu and .gov are often the best first stops for straight facts.

When the Web was new, .com was set aside for commercial sites, .org for nonprofit and charity groups, and .net for Internet service providers.

Good, bad, or irrelevant? When a search turns up dozens of results pages, a quick glance at details like URL tags can save time.

Those designations don't mean so much anymore because just about anyone can use them. Many two-letter URLs indicate foreign countries, such as .ca for Canada; some smaller countries sell or rent theirs out.

If you're on a site for the first time, a quick look around will probably show what they're selling or promoting. Why is the site there in the first place?

After seeing what they want to do, check how they're doing it. Is all the content original? Some of it? Is it a site that collects material from other sites? How can you tell it hasn't been changed? Check original source information at the site where it started.

The next step is to look at the information on the site and ask "Who says?" Reliable writers and producers, no matter what media they work in, choose credible sources and tell who they are. There are three basic ways to tell whether sources are credible:

1. Consider whether the source is in a position to know what he or she is saying.
2. Find out what others think of the source with a name search.
3. Look at what the source has said in the past. Was it accurate?

Verifying the information may be trickier than checking the source. A juicy lie can race from site to site on the Web in seconds. Searching its keywords might turn up several results pages. A fact-checker finding the same information on dozens of sites might conclude that it must be true because so many "sources" are saying the same thing.

The fact-checker might be wrong, though, and so might the information. A single line of disinformation may be cut and pasted or linked everywhere. It may look like dozens of sources are saying the same thing, when only one source is saying it and dozens are repeating it.

Dealing With It

It's one thing to recognize distortion. Deciding what to do with it is something else. It's good practice to note untrustworthy sources and avoid them in the future, and in many cases that's probably enough. Some people, however, resent being deceived and try to get back at liars or scammers, especially if they feel they've been victimized.

An obvious response is to call out liars in blogs and comments. A more effective tactic may be to report the disinformation to a site that specializes in exposing it, such as PolitiFact or, in cases of fraud, the Internet Crime Complaint Center.

"Scambaiting" is using a fake name and address to play along with scammers, wasting their time and resources or getting information to expose them. Trying to trick criminals can get ugly, however, and it isn't recommended. There are several online communities that specialize in baiting, with safety tips.

File   Edit   View   Favorites   Tools   Help

 SAFE SITES FOR CHECKING ON FACTS AND SPIN

Safe Sites for Checking on Facts and Spin

The following Web sites might be useful in checking on facts and their distortion:

FactCheck.org: The nonpartisan Annenberg Public Policy Center's site monitors the accuracy of politicians' and journalists' statements.

Politifact.com: The Tampa Bay Times runs public statements through a "Truth-o-Meter." Results range from "True" to "Pants on Fire." Politifact follows a wide range of people, organizations, and even chain e-mails.

Cdc.gov/nchs: The National Center for Health Statistics (Centers for Disease Control and Prevention) provides data on births, deaths, accidental injuries, and more.

Opensecrets.org: The Center for Responsive Politics tracks lobbying groups and donations to politicians.

Cbo.gov: The Congressional Budget Office is relied on by political parties for objective economic analysis and the possible consequences of new laws.

Bls.gov: The Bureau of Labor Statistics (U.S. Department of Labor) provides official data on jobs, unemployment, wages, and inflation.

Census.gov: The U.S. Census Bureau (U.S. Department of Commerce) provides data on the U.S. population, household income, and other information.

Eia.gov: The U.S. Energy Information Administration (U.S. Department of Energy) provides statistics on gas prices, nuclear power, solar power, and more.

(Continued on page 38)

File   Edit   View   Favorites   Tools   Help

◁   ▷   ↻   ⌂   SAFE SITES FOR CHECKING ON FACTS AND SPIN

Quackwatch.org: Dr. Stephen Barrett founded this respected guide that provides information on health frauds and making intelligent health decisions.

Prwatch.org: The Center for Media and Democracy reports on public relations campaigns and spin by corporations and government agencies, and it promotes citizen journalism.

The best antidote to disinformation is knowing the truth. If you're not certain what the truth is, it helps to know where to find it. Librarians are often the quickest and easiest guide, in person or online. Big institutions like the Library of Congress have an "Ask a Librarian" feature on their sites, and so do many community libraries.

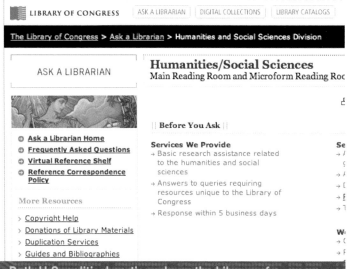

Both U.S. political parties rely on the Library of Congress for straight facts. It's one of many libraries with an online "Ask a Librarian" feature to help students and other researchers.

You Feel Fine? Outrageous!

Everyone lies from time to time, even if it's to say "fine" when asked, "How are you?" when what you really feel is, "I have a headache.

California students take part in an "Ethics Day" discussion. The Web has great fact-finding tools, but only humans can tell what's morally right from wrong.

Leave me alone!" If everyone was perfectly honest, all the time, life would get pretty uncomfortable.

However, just about every society regards lying as something bad. Jews, Christians, and Muslims are commanded not to "bear false witness." True and false are among the great opposites in human thought, as basic as light and dark, knowledge and ignorance, love and hate, good and evil. One way or another, they figure into the moral codes of just about everyone.

Morality and ethics don't disappear in cyberspace. On the Web or on the street, lying is still lying. Digital technology makes it easier and faster to collect and send information, but getting it right still depends on people and on human qualities like fairness, competence, and honesty.

GLOSSARY

bias An inclination to automatically think a certain way; prejudice.

Cold War The hostile relationship between the Soviet Union and the United States, and their allies, that existed between 1945 and 1990.

conflict of interest A situation in which someone has two or more sets of interests or loyalties; a potential abuse of public trust for private gain.

conservative Politics that favor keeping things the same and saving money and resources. Conservatives may favor private and business interests over public interests.

credible Believable; trustworthy or convincing.

discredit To ruin the credibility of something or someone; show to be false.

fascist A right-wing, nationalist form of society or government usually led by a dictator with absolute power.

interest A share in something, such as a business.

left-wing A range of political views and parties that generally support change in hopes of improving society for the greatest number of people. Left-wingers may be moderate, liberal, or go to extremes such as socialism.

liberal Politics that favor change and trying new things, even if they require using money and resources. Liberals generally put public interests ahead of private and business interests.

mainstream media The major broadcast and print corporations that most Americans depend on for news; commercial media.

morality Principles that help people tell the difference between right and wrong or good and bad behavior.

plagiarism The practice of presenting another person's works or ideas as one's own.

prejudice Having an opinion about something before experiencing it, testing it, or reasoning about it.

rhetoric Language that's intended to persuade.

right-wing A range of political views and parties that generally support existing power structures such as states, corporations, armed forces, royalty, and churches. Right-wingers may be moderate, conservative, or go to extremes such as fascism.

spin Describing or interpreting something in a certain way to influence the way people think about it; propaganda.

status quo The present state of affairs.

stereotype A biased way of thinking about a group based on a popular idea about the group.

witch hunt An investigation that harasses or persecutes people instead of looking for real wrongdoing.

FOR MORE INFORMATION

Annenberg Public Policy Center
202 South Thirty-sixth Street
Philadelphia, PA 19104-3806
(215) 898-9400
Web site: http://factcheck.org
The Center's FactCheck.org is a nonprofit, nonpartisan Web site that
    monitors political ads, debates, speeches, press releases, and
    interviews for factual accuracy.

Canadian Journalism Project
59 Adelaide Street E, Suite 500
Toronto ON M5C 1K6
Canada
(416) 955-0394
Web site: http://j-source.ca
The Canadian Journalism Project aims to be a trustworthy source of infor-
    mation and advice on journalism for reporters and readers.

Library of Congress (LOC)
101 Independence Avenue SE
Washington, DC 20540
(202) 707-5000
Web site: http://www.loc.gov
The LOC is home to thousands of pictures, movies, documents, and other
    primary sources in American history. There are huge student
    research sections on the Web site. Visitors can put together their
    own collections. Its THOMAS feature shows how lawmakers vote
    and the full congressional record.

Media Awareness Network
950 Gladstone Avenue, Suite 120
Ottawa, ON K1Y 3E6
Canada
(613) 224-7721
Web site: http://www.media-awareness.ca
Media Awareness Network is a Canadian nonprofit organization that offers information and programs on how media work.

News Literacy Project (NLP)
5525 Devon Road
Bethesda, MD 20814
(301) 651-7499
Web site: http://www.thenewsliteracyproject.org
The NLP sponsors programs for middle school and high school students to help them sort fact from fiction in digital media. Seasoned journalists discuss critical thinking skills and how to distinguish facts from opinion and spin.

Poynter Institute
801 Third Street South
St. Petersburg, FL 33701
(727) 821-9494
Web site: http://www.poynter.org
The Poynter Institute is widely respected for its journalism instruction programs, including online courses for student journalists, bloggers, and citizen journalists.

Web Sites

Due to the changing nature of Internet links, Rosen Publishing has developed an online list of Web sites related to the subject of this book. This site is updated regularly. Please use this link to access the list:

http://www.rosenlinks.com/DIL/Facts

FOR FURTHER READING

Badke, William. *Research Strategies: Finding Your Way Through the Information Fog*. Lincoln, NE: iUniverse, 2008.

Campbell, Richard, Christopher R. Martin, and Bettina Fabos. *Media and Culture: An Introduction to Mass Communication*. Boston, MA: Bedford/St. Martin's, 2012.

Cooper, Sheila, and Rosemary Patton. *Writing Logically, Thinking Critically*. 6th ed. New York, NY: Longman Publishing Group, 2009.

George, Mary W. *The Elements of Library Research: What Every Student Needs to Know*. Princeton, NJ: Princeton University Press, 2008.

Gerber, Larry. *Cited! Identifying Credible Information Online* (Digital and Information Literacy). New York, NY: Rosen Publishing Group, 2011.

Hoyle, Russ. *Going to War: How Misinformation, Disinformation, and Arrogance Led America into Iraq*. New York, NY: St. Martin's Press, 2008.

Lester, James D. *Writing Research Papers: A Complete Guide*. 13th ed. New York, NY: Longman Publishing Group, 2009.

Orwell, George. *1984*. London, England: Secker and Warburg, 1949.

Robinson, Tom. *The Evolution of News Reporting* (Essential Viewpoints). San Francisco, CA: Essential Library, 2010.

Skog, Jason. *Yellow Journalism*. Mankato, MN: Capstone Press. 2007.

Steven, Peter. *The News: A Groundwork Guide*. Toronto, ON, Canada: Groundwood Books, 2010.

Warlick, David. *Classroom Blogging*. 2nd ed. Morrisville, NC: Lulu.com, 2007.

Weston, Anthony. *A Rulebook for Arguments*. 4th ed. Indianapolis IN: Hackett Publishing, 2009.

Anti-Phishing Working Group. "Consumer Advice: How to Avoid Phishing Scams." Retrieved April 28, 2012 (http://www.antiphishing.org/consumer_recs.html).

Brockman, John, ed. *Culture Leading Scientists Explore Societies, Art, Power, and Technology.* New York, NY: HarperCollins, 2011.

Brooks, Brian S., George Kennedy, Daryl R. Moen, and Don Ranly. *Telling the Story Writing for Print, Broadcast and Online Media.* Boston, MA: Bedford/St. Martin's, 2001.

Farsetta, Diane. "Fake TV News: Widespread and Undisclosed." Center for Media and Democracy, March 16, 2006. Retrieved May 27, 2012 (http://www.prwatch.org/fakenews/execsummary).

Federal Bureau of Investigation Uniform Crime Reports. "Crime in the United States: Violent Crime." Retrieved May 18, 2012 (http://www.fbi.gov/about-us/cjis/ucr/crime-in-the-u.s/2010/crime-in-the-u.s.-2010/violent-crime).

Hanley, Charles J. "Half of U.S. Still Believes Iraq Had WMD." *Washington Post*, August 7, 2006. Retrieved May 26, 2012 (http://www.washingtonpost.com/wp-dyn/content/article/2006/08/07/AR2006080700189.html).

Jackson, Brooks, and Jamieson, Kathleen. *unSpun Finding Facts in a World of Disinformation.* New York, NY: Random House, 2007.

Kumar, Deepa. "Media, War, and Propaganda: Strategies of Information Management During the 2003 Iraq War." *Communication and Critical/Cultural Studies*, Vol. 3, No. 1, March 2006, pp. 48–69. Retrieved May 26, 2012 (comminfo.rutgers.edu/~dkumar/Articles/iraqwar.pdf).

Lindsay, Don. "A List of Fallacious Arguments." May 6, 2012. Retrieved May 24, 2012 (http://www.don-lindsay-archive.org/skeptic/arguments.html).

Lisciotto, Carmelo. "Julius Streicher: The Beast of Franconia." The Holocaust Research Project. Retrieved April 25, 2012 (http://www.holocaustresearchproject.org/holoprelude/streicher.html).

Mikkelsen, Randall. "CIA, FBI Computers Used for Wikipedia Edits." Reuters, August 16, 2007. Retrieved May 18, 2012 (http://forum.prisonplanet.com/index.php?topic=1641.msg6146#msg6146).

Naureckas, Jim. "The Military-Editorial Complex." Fairness & Accuracy in Reporting, October 1995. Retrieved April 27, 2012 (http://www.fair.org/index.php?page=1327).

Parry, Robert. "How the U.S. Press Lost Its Way." *Consortium News*, May 16, 2012. Retrieved May 18, 2012 (http://readersupportednews.org/opinion2/276-74/11454-how-the-us-press-lost-its-way).

Pew Research Center. "Strong Support for Watchdog Role, Despite Public Criticism of News Media." October 2, 2009. Retrieved May 17, 2012 (http://pewresearch.org/pubs/1364/strong-support-for-watchdog-role-despite-public-criticism-of-news-media).

Potter, Deborah. "Training Citizen Journalists." NewsLab, October 27, 2009. Retrieved May 16, 2012 (http://www.newslab.org/2009/10/27/training-citizen-journalists).

Shuttleworth, Martyn. "Asch Experiment." Experiment Resources. Retrieved May 12, 2012 (http://www.experiment-resources.com/asch-experiment.html).

Ulick, Terry, and Alyssa Wodtke. *Truth, Lies, and Online Dating*. Boston, MA: Thompson, 2005.

INDEX

About the Author

Larry Gerber is a former Associated Press bureau chief who has reported news and trained journalists in Europe, Asia, and the United States. Gerber is also author of *Cited! Identifying Credible Information Online*. He lives in Los Angeles, California.

Photo Credits

Designer: Nicole Russo; Editor: Kathy Kuhtz Campbell;
Photo Researcher: Amy Feinberg